Women's Suffrage

Fighting for Women's Rights

Harriet Isecke

Consultant

Marcus McArthur, Ph.D.
Department of History
Saint Louis University

Publishing Credits

Dona Herweck Rice, *Editor-in-Chief*
Lee Aucoin, *Creative Director*
Chris McIntyre, M.A.Ed., *Editorial Director*
Torrey Maloof, *Associate Editor*
Neri Garcia, *Senior Designer*
Stephanie Reid, *Photo Researcher*
Rachelle Cracchiolo, M.S.Ed., *Publisher*

Image Credits

cover Hulton Archive/Getty Images; p.1 Hulton Archive/Getty Images; p.4 The Library of Congress; p.5 (left) The Library of Congress; p.5 (right) The Library of Congress; p.6 (top) The Library of Congress; p.6 (bottom) The Library of Congress; p.7 (top) The Library of Congress; p.7 (bottom) The Library of Congress; p.8 *History of Woman Suffrage*, 1881/Google Books; p.9 The Library of Congress; p.11 (top, left) The Library of Congress; p.11 (right) The Granger Collection, New York; p.11 (bottom, left) The Library of Congress; p.12 The Library of Congress; p.13 (top) The Library of Congress; p.13 (bottom) The Library of Congress; p.14 The Library of Congress; p.15 (top) The Granger Collection, New York; p.15 (bottom) National Archives; p.16 The Library of Congress; p.17 National Archives; p.18 The Library of Congress; p.19 HultonArchive/iStockphoto; p.20 The Library of Congress; p.21 (top) The Library of Congress; p.21 (bottom) The Library of Congress; p.22 Corbis; p.23 (top) The Library of Congress; p.23 (bottom) The Library of Congress; p.24 (top) The Library of Congress; p.24 (bottom) The Library of Congress; p.25 (top) The Library of Congress; p.25 (bottom) The Library of Congress; p.27 (top) The Library of Congress; p.27 (bottom) The Library of Congress; p.29 (top) National Archives; p.29 (bottom) The Library of Congress; p.32 (left) The Library of Congress; p.32 (right) The Library of Congress

---

Teacher Created Materials
5301 Oceanus Drive
Huntington Beach, CA 92649-1030
http://www.tcmpub.com

ISBN 978-1-4333-1507-7

Table of Contents

The Fight for Rights

Did you know that when the United States was founded, women did not have the same rights as men? Women could not own **property**. Women could not attend most colleges. They were not allowed to do many of the same jobs that men did. And, when they did work the same jobs, men were paid more for the same work.

Some women accepted these rules and made the best of their lives. Others fought for more rights and opportunities. They fought to change the laws. A little bit at a time, they started succeeding. Women were slowly given more rights. But, there was still one big right that they did not have. Women still could not vote.

Suffragists on parade in New York City in 1912

A suffragist poster

Mary Wollstonecraft

Famous First

One of the first women to write about women's rights was Mary Wollstonecraft. She was from England. In 1792, she wrote a famous book called *A **Vindication** of the Rights of Woman*. In her book, Wollstonecraft said men and women should be equal.

All Men Are Created Equal

John Adams signed the Declaration of Independence in 1776. His wife, Abigail, requested that he and the other men "remember the ladies." By this, she meant to give women the same rights as men.

The fight to change the law to allow women to vote was called the **Suffrage** (SUHF-rij) Movement. Those who joined this fight were called **suffragists**. Many brave suffragists organized groups, gave speeches, and held marches and parades. It took women almost 150 years to get the right to vote. This is the story of how they did it.

The Movement Begins

Elizabeth Cady Stanton Meets Lucretia Mott

Elizabeth Cady Stanton

In 1840, a young Elizabeth Cady Stanton left for England. She was on her way to an antislavery **convention** in London. When she arrived at the convention, she was shocked. She learned that the British **abolitionists** (ab-uh-LISH-uh-nists) had decided that no woman would be able to participate in the convention. Women would not be allowed to speak, and they would have to sit in a separate area.

It was at this convention that Cady Stanton met Lucretia (loo-KREE-shuh) Mott. Mott was a famous abolitionist. She fought hard to end slavery. She was also a firm believer in equal rights for women. Mott wanted women to be able to own property. She wanted them to have equal opportunities for a good education and good jobs. She also wanted women to have legal **custody** of their children. At that time, only men had legal rights to children.

Lucretia Mott

Cady Stanton and Mott decided they would hold a convention to discuss women's rights. In 1848, the first Woman's Rights Convention was held in Seneca Falls, New York. Both women and men came to the convention. They talked about ways to improve the lives of women.

THE FIRST CONVENTION

EVER CALLED TO DISCUSS THE

Civil and Political Rights of Women,

SENECA FALLS, N. Y., JULY 19, 20, 1848.

WOMAN'S RIGHTS CONVENTION.

A Convention to discuss the social, civil, and religious condition and rights of woman will be held in the Wesleyan Chapel, at Seneca Falls, N. Y., on Wednesday and Thursday, the 19th and 20th of July current; commencing at 10 o'clock A. M. During the first day the meeting will be exclusively for women, who are earnestly invited to attend. The public generally are invited to be present on the second day, when Lucretia Mott, of Philadelphia, and other ladies and gentlemen, will address the Convention.*

* This call was published in the *Seneca County Courier*, July 14, 1848, without any signatures. The movers of this Convention, who drafted the call, the declaration and resolutions were Elizabeth Cady Stanton, Lucretia Mott, Martha C. Wright, Mary Ann McClintock, and Jane C. Hunt.

A published invitation to attend the first Woman's Rights Convention

Frederick Douglass

And Women...

At the Woman's Rights Convention, Elizabeth Cady Stanton read to the crowd a special paper she had written. It was called the *Declaration of Sentiments*. It was based on the Declaration of Independence. But, Cady Stanton's declaration said that "all men and women are created equal." It described the **plight** of women. It talked about how poorly women were treated by men. It said that women could not get a good education, get good jobs, or own property. It demanded that women be given the right to vote.

Famous Guest

One of the men who attended the Woman's Rights Convention was Frederick Douglass. He was a famous abolitionist. He fought against slavery. He also fought for women's rights. Douglass had been a slave so he knew what it was like not to have any civil rights. The abolitionists and the suffragists worked together for many years.

Susan B. Anthony Joins the Movement

Susan B. Anthony

Susan B. Anthony's father wanted all his children, including his daughters, to go to school. The Anthonys were part of the religious group called the **Quakers** (KWEY-kerz). Quakers believed that women and men should be treated equally. But, the local school would not let girls attend. So, Anthony's father set up a school at home. Anthony later became a teacher. She taught for ten years.

Anthony found out that the male teachers made four times her salary. She tried to get equal pay, but did not succeed. Anthony quit teaching and worked for the **Temperance** Movement. Members of the Temperance Movement wanted to reduce, or limit, the sale and use of alcohol. Anthony believed alcohol was destroying families.

In 1853, Anthony attended a temperance meeting in New York. When she tried to speak at the meeting, Anthony was told that women were only allowed to listen and learn. They were not allowed to speak. This angered Anthony. A few years earlier, Anthony had met Cady Stanton. She decided it was time to ask her new friend for help. Together they started their own temperance group.

Anthony and Cady Stanton continued to work together for the rest of their lives. Cady Stanton was a deep thinker and a great writer. Anthony was a great organizer. Together they fought for women's rights.

A suffragist poster

Mary Wollstonecraft

The fight to change the law to allow women to vote was called the **Suffrage** (SUHF-rij) Movement. Those who joined this fight were called **suffragists**. Many brave suffragists organized groups, gave speeches, and held marches and parades. It took women almost 150 years to get the right to vote. This is the story of how they did it.

Famous First

One of the first women to write about women's rights was Mary Wollstonecraft. She was from England. In 1792, she wrote a famous book called ***A Vindication of the Rights of Woman***. In her book, Wollstonecraft said men and women should be equal.

All Men Are Created Equal

John Adams signed the Declaration of Independence in 1776. His wife, Abigail, requested that he and the other men "remember the ladies." By this, she meant to give women the same rights as men.

The Movement Begins

Elizabeth Cady Stanton Meets Lucretia Mott

Elizabeth Cady Stanton

In 1840, a young Elizabeth Cady Stanton left for England. She was on her way to an antislavery **convention** in London. When she arrived at the convention, she was shocked. She learned that the British **abolitionists** (ab-uh-LISH-uh-nists) had decided that no woman would be able to participate in the convention. Women would not be allowed to speak, and they would have to sit in a separate area.

It was at this convention that Cady Stanton met Lucretia (loo-KREE-shuh) Mott. Mott was a famous abolitionist. She fought hard to end slavery. She was also a firm believer in equal rights for women. Mott wanted women to be able to own property. She wanted them to have equal opportunities for a good education and good jobs. She also wanted women to have legal **custody** of their children. At that time, only men had legal rights to children.

Lucretia Mott

Cady Stanton and Mott decided they would hold a convention to discuss women's rights. In 1848, the first Woman's Rights Convention was held in Seneca Falls, New York. Both women and men came to the convention. They talked about ways to improve the lives of women.

Anthony's Absence

Anthony did not go to the Woman's Rights Convention in Seneca Falls. At the time, she thought the convention was silly. When she was told about it, she laughed. But after the members of the Temperance Movement treated Anthony unfairly, she quickly changed her mind.

It Takes Two

Cady Stanton was good at writing speeches. Anthony considered Cady Stanton the "brains" of the movement. And she thought of herself as its "hands and feet." Anthony would organize all the conventions, raise funds, give speeches, and get **petitions** signed. Anthony would also babysit Cady Stanton's children so that she could focus on her writing. Cady Stanton had seven children when she met Anthony!

Temperance Movement poster

I Will Wear What I Want

Amelia Jenks Bloomer attended the Woman's Rights Convention at Seneca Falls and was eager to help the Suffrage Movement. Bloomer was against slavery and alcohol. She wrote about these issues and how they affected women. Bloomer also ran her own newspaper called *The Lily*.

In 1851, Bloomer would become known more for her clothing than her newspaper. At that time, women wore tight underclothing that made it hard for them to move freely. Bloomer started wearing loose pants that were gathered at the ankle under shorter dresses. These outfits were more comfortable and made it easier for women to move around. Bloomer loved this new style of dress and wrote about it in her newspaper.

The writers at the *New York Tribune* newspaper saw what Bloomer had written about the new style of clothing and they wrote about it, too. The pants were nicknamed *bloomers*. The **majority** of the public disapproved of this new look. But, many women felt it was their right to wear what they wanted to wear.

Where Did Bloomers Come From?

Cady Stanton's cousin, Elizabeth Smith Miller created bloomers. She wanted a practical dress. When Cady Stanton saw how easily her cousin was able to move and work in these new dresses, she started wearing them, too. The short dresses quickly became the uniform for women suffragists! They also became a symbol for women's rights.

No More Bloomers

The bloomers trend did not last long. Many people disapproved of the new style of dress because they thought it looked too much like men's pants. Others started laughing at women for wearing bloomers. Many articles were written making fun of the new style. The women in the Suffrage Movement thought that bloomers might hurt their cause. By 1854, most women had stopped wearing bloomers, including Amelia Bloomer.

THE LILY.

DEVOTED TO THE INTERESTS OF WOMAN.

AMELIA BLOOMER, EDITOR AND PUBLISHER.—ISSUED SEMI-MONTHLY AT FIFTY CENTS A YEAR IN ADVANCE.

SENECA FALLS, N. Y., JUNE 15, 1853.

Bloomer's newspaper focused on the interests of women.

Amelia Jenks Bloomer

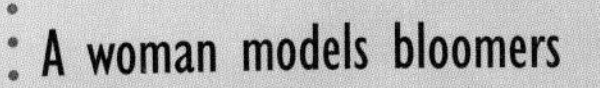

A woman models bloomers

The Fight to Own Property

In the early 1800s, most states did not let married women own property. If a woman had money of her own, it became her husband's once she got married. A woman's husband owned and controlled everything that was hers. Cady Stanton and Anthony wanted this to change. The women decided to fight for women's property rights in the state of New York.

Anthony was not married, so she had more time to run the campaign. Cady Stanton did the research and writing. The fight was not easy and took a lot of work. Anthony spoke in 54 counties. She was met by angry **mobs** that said that women should be in the home and not making speeches on the streets.

Cady Stanton gave a powerful speech to the New York **legislature** (LEJ-is-ley-cher) in which she explained to the lawmakers why women needed these rights. The speech worked! The lawmakers changed their minds. In 1860, a new law passed. Married women were finally able to own their own property!

Cady Stanton with one of her children

Some men were not happy about women getting rights, so they started forming antisuffrage groups.

This cartoon shows what some people thought would happen if women got more rights.

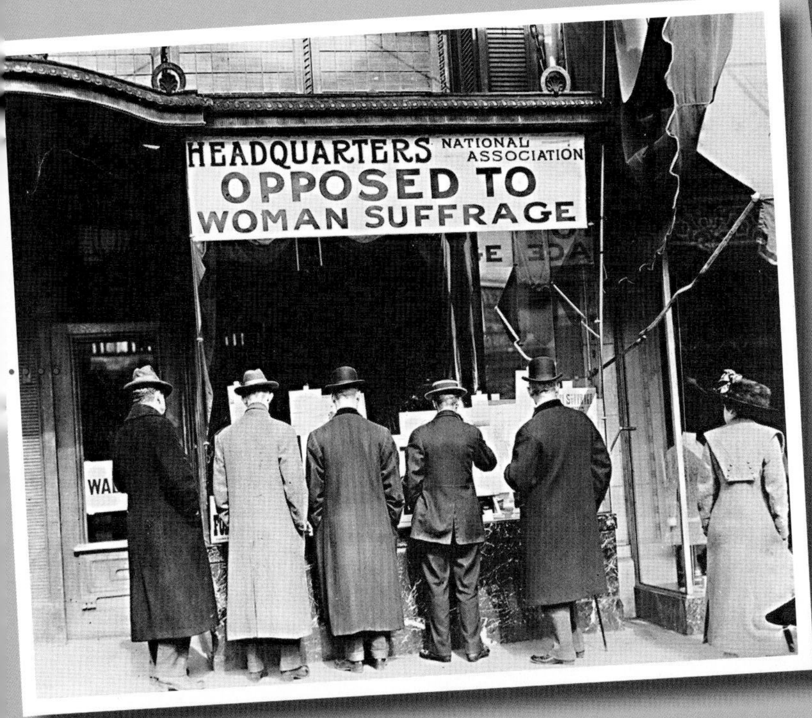

More Rights

The new law that passed in 1860 gave New York women more rights than they had ever had before. If a woman had a job and was earning money, she could now keep that money for herself. Women could also **sue** and be sued in a court of law. And, women could now own their own property.

Custody Rights

Women did not always have the legal right to make decisions regarding their children. If a husband and wife separated or divorced, the man had legal rights to the children. The new law that passed in 1860 changed that for the women of New York. It gave them shared custody rights. They now had a say in what happened to their children. Unfortunately, this new right was quickly taken back. In 1862, the New York legislature abolished, or repealed, this part of the law.

Lucy Stone

Who Is Right?

Lucy Stone was a suffragist who thought that free African American men should have rights before women. Both Cady Stanton and Anthony strongly disagreed. Mott was the peacemaker. She tried to get the two sides to understand each other.

The Fourteenth Amendment

In 1868, the Fourteenth Amendment to the United States Constitution was passed. This amendment gave African American men equal rights, but it did not include women. It also did not include the right to vote.

Let Us Vote!

Antislavery and Suffrage Groups Disagree

From 1861 to 1865, the Civil War raged in the United States. The Southern states wanted to leave the **Union** over the right to own slaves. The Northern states wanted to keep the United States together. Much of the time and attention that had been spent on women's rights were now focused on the war.

When the Civil War ended, the Thirteenth **Amendment** to the United States Constitution was passed. This ended slavery in the United States. But, free African American men still did not have the same rights as white men. Neither did women.

In 1866, both antislavery and prosuffrage groups met at the National Woman's Rights Convention. Cady Stanton and Anthony spoke at the convention. They wanted the two groups to work together. They thought they could help each other. A new group was formed. It was called the American Equal Rights Association (AERA).

Women did not have a lot of time during the Civil War to focus on the Suffrage Movement. These women are helping to make bullets for the war.

Thirty-Eighth Congress of the United States of America;

At the Second Session,

Begun and held at the City of Washington, on Monday, the fifth day of December, one thousand eight hundred and sixty-four

A RESOLUTION

Submitting to the legislatures of the several States a proposition to amend the Constitution of the United States.

Resolved by the Senate and House of Representatives of the United States of America in Congress assembled, (two-thirds of both houses concurring), that the following article be proposed to the legislatures of the several States as an amendment to the Constitution of the United States, which, when ratified by three-fourths of said legislatures shall be valid, to all intents and purposes, as a part of the said Constitution, namely: Article XIII. Section 1. Neither slavery nor involuntary servitude, except as a punishment for crime whereof the party shall have been duly convicted, shall exist within the United States, or any place subject to their jurisdiction. Section 2. Congress shall have power to enforce this article by appropriate legislation.

Schuyler Colfax
Speaker of the House of Representatives.

H. Hamlin
Vice President of the United States and President of the Senate

Approved, February 1. 1865.

Abraham Lincoln

PRIVATE LAWS

The Thirteenth Amendment ended slavery in America.

A Bad Split

It was now 1869, and trouble was brewing. African American men still did not have the right to vote. And, neither did women. Then the Fifteenth Amendment was proposed. This would give free African American men the right to vote. Some thought this was unfair and that women should be included, too. Others thought that women should have to wait.

Cady Stanton and Anthony asked the AERA to fight to include women in the Fifteenth Amendment. They wanted it to call for **universal** suffrage. But, the AERA voted to let it stand as written. This created a lot of tension in the group and caused it to split.

This print celebrates the Fifteenth Amendment.

A PETITION

FOR

UNIVERSAL SUFFRAGE.

To the Senate and House of Representatives:

The undersigned, Women of the United States, respectfully ask an amendment of the Constitution that shall prohibit the several States from disfranchising any of their citizens on the ground of sex.

In making our demand for Suffrage, we would call your attention to the fact that we represent fifteen million people—one half the entire population of the country—intelligent, virtuous, native-born American citizens; and yet stand outside the pale of political recognition.

The Constitution classes us as "free people," and counts us *whole* persons in the basis of representation; and yet are we governed without our consent, compelled to pay taxes without appeal, and punished for violations of law without choice of judge or juror.

The experience of all ages, the Declarations of the Fathers, the Statute Laws of our own day, and the fearful revolution through which we have just passed, all prove the uncertain tenure of life, liberty and property so long as the ballot—the only weapon of self-protection—is not in the hand of every citizen.

Therefore, as you are now amending the Constitution, and, in harmony with advancing civilization, placing new safeguards round the individual rights of four millions of emancipated slaves, we ask that you extend the right of Suffrage to Woman—the only remaining class of disfranchised citizens—and thus fulfil your Constitutional obligation "to Guarantee to every State in the Union a Republican form of Government."

As all partial application of Republican principles must ever breed a complicated legislation as well as a discontented people, we would pray your Honorable Body, in order to simplify the machinery of government and ensure domestic tranquillity, that you legislate hereafter for persons, citizens, tax-payers, and not for class or caste.

For justice and equality your petitioners will ever pray.

NAMES.	RESIDENCE.
E. Cady Stanton.	New York
Susan B. Anthony	Rochester — N.Y.
Antoinette Brown Blackwell	New York
Lucy Stone	Newark N. Jersey
Joanna S. Morse	48 Livingston St. Brooklyn
Ernestine L. Rose	New York
Harriet E. Eaton	6. West 14th Street N.Y.
Catharine C. Wilkeson	83 Clinton Place New York
Elizabeth R. Tilton	48 Livingston St. Brooklyn
Mary Fowler Gilbert	293 W. 19th St New York
Mary E. Gilbert	New York
M. Griffith	New York

This petition asks for voting rights for everyone, including women. It is signed by Cady Stanton and Anthony.

Anthony and Cady Stanton started a new group called the National Woman Suffrage Association (NWSA). They focused on voting rights for women. They thought African American men, as well as all women, should get the right to vote at the same time.

Lucy Stone helped start another group called the American Woman Suffrage Association (AWSA). This group supported the Fifteenth Amendment the way it was written. It thought that the Fifteenth Amendment would not pass if women were included.

The Fifteenth Amendment

On February 3, 1870, the Fifteenth Amendment to the United States Constitution was passed. African American men now had the right to vote. But, just as Cady Stanton had feared, women were still not allowed to vote. They had not been included in the amendment.

The Woman's Journal

In 1873, Lucy Stone started *The Woman's Journal*. This was the publication for her group, the American Woman Suffrage Association (AWSA). Later, her daughter, Alice Stone Blackwell, wrote a book about her called *Lucy Stone: Pioneer of Woman's Rights.*

No Votes for Women

The case that went to the Supreme Court in 1875 was *Minor vs. Happersett*. Virginia Minor said that the Fourteenth Amendment gave her the right to vote. The Supreme Court voted unanimously against Minor. That means that all the judges agreed. They said women did not have the right to vote under the United States Constitution. The ruling said each state would have to decide who would be allowed to vote.

Victoria Woodhull

Victoria Woodhull was the one who came up with the idea to use the Fourteenth Amendment as proof that women could legally vote. But, her argument did not work. Woodhull then decided to run for president in 1872. She wanted to prove how ridiculous it was that women could legally run for president of the United States, but could not vote in the presidential election.

THE WOMAN WHO DARED.

Close of the Trial of Susan B. Anthony.

OPINION AND DECISION OF JUDGE HUNT.

The Fourteenth Amendment Gives No Right to a Woman to Vote.

MISS ANTHONY'S ACT A VIOLATION OF LAW.

Exhaustive Opinion on the Force and Scope of the Amendments.

A VERDICT OF GUILTY.

The Champion of Woman's Rights Awaiting Sentence and Martyrdom.

CANANDAIGUA, N. Y., June 18, 1873.

The court room was again thronged this morning at the hour of opening by an attentive audience as spectators in the further progress of the trial of Miss Anthony.

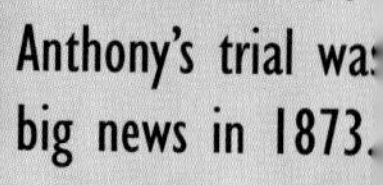

Anthony's trial was big news in 1873.

Woodhull campaigns for the presidency in 1872.

Breaking the Law

By 1872, suffragists were getting impatient. Soon there would be a presidential election. Maybe the Fourteenth Amendment to the United States Constitution could help women after all. The first **article** in the amendment said that no state could **deny** any person "equal protection." Maybe that meant that women could vote. Some brave women decided to try it.

Anthony got 50 women in Rochester, New York to vote. At least 100 other women voted across the United States. Anthony went to the polls, but the men would not let her vote. So, she threatened to sue them. Finally, they let her vote.

A few weeks later, Anthony was arrested for voting **illegally**. Her trial was unfair. The entire jury was made up of men because women were not allowed to be jurors in New York. And, the judge ordered the jury to find Anthony guilty.

Another case about women voting did reach the United States **Supreme Court**. Women everywhere were waiting to hear the verdict. The court said "equal protection" did not mean that women could vote. After that, the suffragists decided not to fight in the **federal courts** anymore. Instead, they would fight in individual states and in Congress.

State by State

By 1870, there were two states that had given women the right to vote: Wyoming and Utah. But in 1872, South Dakota voted against women's suffrage by three votes. And in 1874, Michigan did not have enough votes for women's suffrage, either.

One of the biggest **opponents** for women's rights was the Liquor (LIK-er) **Lobby**. The Liquor Lobby fought hard against the women's vote. They thought that if women could vote, they would want to **ban** the sale of liquor, or alcohol. In 1882, men in Nebraska and Indiana voted against giving women in their states the right to vote. The liquor lobby was just too strong in those states.

Things continued to go up and down. In 1883, the state of Washington allowed women to vote. But, this did not last long. In 1887, the Supreme Court changed the law and said they could not vote there. Congress decided women could not vote in Utah either. But later, in 1896, women were allowed to vote in Utah.

Women voting in Wyoming in 1888

This cartoon shows the progress of women's rights state by state.

This map shows the states in which women could vote by the year 1917.

A Small Victory

Women had a small victory in Michigan and Minnesota. Women were not allowed to vote in city, state, or federal elections. But, they could vote in school elections.

No More Alcohol

In 1875, Anthony gave a speech about the problems alcohol caused for women. She argued that because women had to depend on men for food and shelter, men should not be allowed to waste all their time and money on drinking. She said that while men are busy drinking, their wives and children suffer. Anthony wanted equal rights for women so that they could take care of themselves and their children without having to be dependent on men.

Worldwide Problem

The United States was not the only country where women were denied rights. Women all over the world did not have equal rights. In 1882, Cady Stanton and Anthony went to Europe. They met with women there and planned a huge conference, or meeting. The conference was to take place on the **anniversary** of the first Woman's Rights Convention. That convention was held in Seneca Falls, New York, 40 years earlier.

The first International Council of Women (ICW) conference was held in Washington, DC, in 1888. It was the biggest meeting of its time. Women came from all over the world. The ICW wanted to start a special women's group in each country. These groups would then work together toward the same goal: equal rights for women.

The ICW did not work out the way Cady Stanton and Anthony had hoped. Women in other countries failed either to start or keep their groups going. But, one great thing did happen. The two main suffrage groups from the United States started to work together again. And in 1890, these two groups joined as one. The new group was called the National American Woman Suffrage Association (NAWSA).

The women who arranged the International Council of Women conference

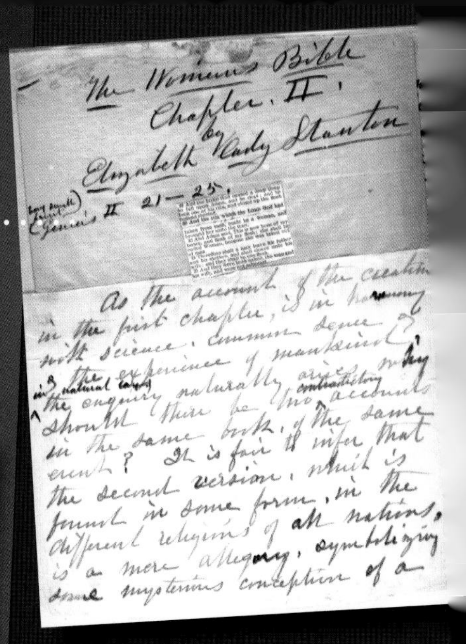
The Woman's Bible
Chapter. II.
by
Elizabeth Cady Stanton
Genesis II 21—25.

As the account of the creation in the first chapter, is in harmony with science, common sense, & the experience of mankind in natural laws, the enquiry naturally arises, why should there be two contradictory accounts in the same book, of the same event? It is fair to infer that the second version, which is found in some form, in the different religions of all nations, is a mere allegory, symbolizing some mysterious conception of a

Cady Stanton's original notes for *The Woman's Bible.*

A Bible for Women

In 1892, Cady Stanton decided to change the Bible. She thought parts of it made women look bad. She worked with other women to write *The Woman's Bible*. The writers changed parts of the Bible to make women stronger. The NAWSA thought that this was a terrible idea. They thought it would hurt their cause. That same year, Cady Stanton was removed from her spot as president of the NAWSA.

International Meeting

The women that attended the ICW conference came from many different places, including Canada, Norway, England, Ireland, Scotland, France, and Finland.

International Council of Women (ICW) Suffrage Conference flyer

Passing the Torch

Alice Paul and Carrie Chapman Catt

Alice Paul

Carrie Chapman Catt

Two of the most important leaders in the suffrage movement were getting older. Despite her age, Cady Stanton kept up the fight by continuing to write articles about the plight of women. Sadly, she died in 1902.

Anthony was heartbroken when her friend died, but she did not give up. Anthony continued to fight for women's rights. When she was 86 years old, she spoke to the NAWSA for the last time. She said that she was sure the suffrage movement would achieve its goal soon. She said, "Failure is impossible." Anthony died a few weeks later. Now it was up to new brave leaders like Alice Paul and Carrie Chapman Catt to carry the torch.

Paul was a **militant** leader. She took a strong stand for women's rights and would not back down. She often put herself at risk. Paul wanted to concentrate on changing the federal law.

Catt and the NAWSA still wanted to work state by state for women's suffrage. So, Paul and others broke off from the NAWSA and formed a new group. Later, that group became the National Woman's Party (NWP).

Emmeline Pankhurst

Some suffragists who refused to eat in prison were force-fed through a tube.

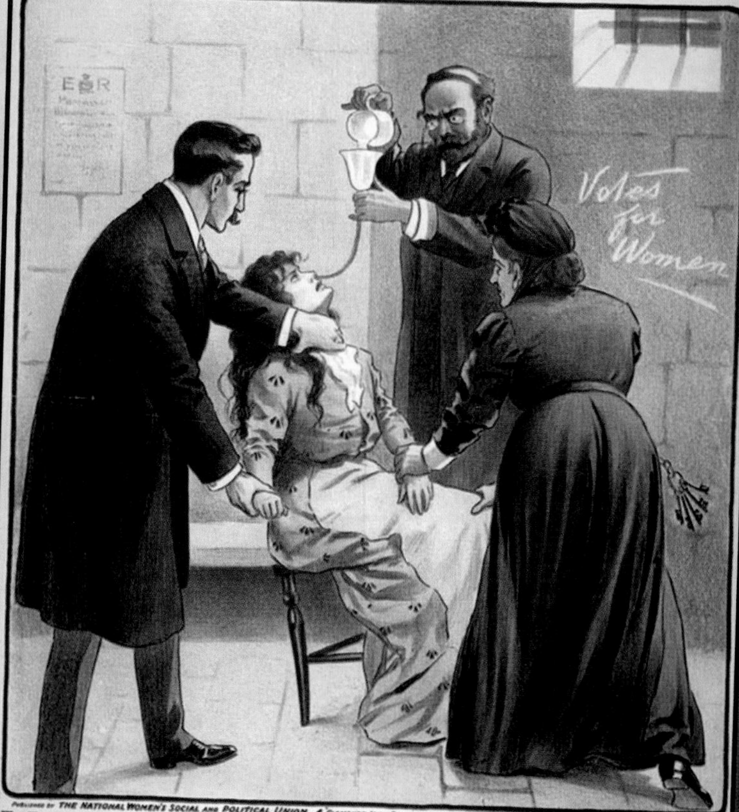

Across the Pond

Across the Atlantic Ocean in Britain, women suffragists were fighting hard for the right to vote, too. A woman named Emmeline Pankhurst was one of the leaders in Britain's Suffrage Movement. The women in her organization were more radical, or extreme, than those in the United States. They were known for fighting police officers and breaking windows.

Taking a Strong Stand

Alice Paul lived in Britain and participated in the Suffrage Movement there. She learned many **tactics** from the British suffragists. She joined in **hunger strikes** and protests. When she returned to the United States, she used these strategies. As a result, she ended up in prison three times.

Another Try

One month after the Woman's Suffrage Parade, Paul organized support for the "Susan B. Anthony" Amendment. It was brought to Congress in 1914. It did not get the two-thirds vote it needed. But, it did get a majority of the votes at 35 to 34.

Off to Jail!

Paul believed that President Wilson had promised to support women's suffrage in 1913. She was angry that in 1917 when he was re-elected, the amendment still had not passed. She organized women to **picket** the White House. Paul and other protesters were arrested.

Women's Suffrage Parade

In 1913, Woodrow Wilson was elected president of the United States. President Wilson arrived in Washington, DC, on March 3, one day before his **inauguration** (in-aw-gyuh-REY-shun). He expected to see crowds of people cheering him on. Half a million people came to Washington. But, very few people came to see the new president—they had come to see a Woman's Suffrage Parade.

Paul and her friend Lucy Barnes organized the parade. They thought it would help get an amendment passed that would allow women to vote. Over 5,000 women marched in the parade.

Some people in the crowd were angry. They yelled at the marchers. Others spit at the women. Some of the women were beaten and over 200 were injured. Even though they had a **permit** for the parade, most of the policemen did nothing to protect the women.

Many people were angry because of the violence. They demanded an **investigation**. The police chief was fired. There was now new sympathy for the women of the Suffrage Movement.

WOMAN'S JOURNAL AND SUFFRAGE NEWS

VOL. XLIV. NO. 10 — SATURDAY, MARCH 8, 1913 — FIVE CENTS

PARADE STRUGGLES TO VICTORY DESPITE DISGRACEFUL SCENES

Nation Aroused by Open Insults to Women—Cause Wins Popular Sympathy—Congress Orders Investigation—Striking Object Lesson

Washington has been disgraced. Equal suffrage has scored a great victory. Thousands of indifferent women have been aroused. Influential men are incensed and the United States Senate demands an investigation of the treatment given the suffragists at the National Capital on Monday.

Ten thousand women from all over the country had planned a magnificent parade and pageant to take place in Washington on March 3. Artists, pageant leaders, designers, women of influence and renown were ready to give a wonderful and beautiful piece of suffrage work to the public that would throng the National Capital for the inauguration festivities. The suffragists were ready; the whole procession started down Pennsylvania avenue, when the police protection, that had been promised, failed them, and a disgraceful scene followed. The crowd surged into the space which had been marked off for the paraders, and the leaders of the suffrage movement were compelled to push their way through a mob of the worst element in Washington and vicinity. Women were spit upon, slapped in the face, tripped up, pelted with burning cigar stubs, and insulted by jeers and obscene language too vile to print or repeat.

The cause of all the trouble is apparent when the facts are known. The police authorities in Washington opposed every attempt to have a suffrage parade at all. Having been forbidden a place in the inaugural procession, the suffragists asked to have a procession of their own on March 3. They were finally told that they could have a procession but that it could not be on Pennsylvania avenue, but must be on a side street. At last they got permission to have the suffrage parade on the avenue, and asked that traffic be excluded from the street during the parade. For a long time this was denied, and only on Saturday were they successful.

Everything was at last arranged; it was a glorious day; ten thousand women were ready to do their part to make the parade beautiful to behold, to make it a credit to womanhood and to demonstrate the strength of the movement for their enfranchisement.

The police were determined, however, and they had their way. Their attempt to afford the marchers protection and keep the space of the avenue free for the suffrage procession was the flimsiest sham. Police officers stood by with folded arms and grinned while the picked women of the land were insulted and roughly abused by an ignorant and uncouth mob.

Miss Alice Paul and other suffragists were compelled to drive their automobiles down the avenue to separate the crowds so the suffragists with the banners and floats could pass. The police officials say their force was inadequate to handle the crowds, but it is noted that there was no disorder on the avenue during the inaugural procession. It is stated that federal troops were offered to the chief of police for the suffrage procession, but that he refused their aid. At any rate, assistance was finally called from Fort Myer and mounted soldiers drove back the crowd so that a straggling line of marchers could pass through.

Not only were the suffragists bitterly disappointed in having the effect

(Continued on Page 78)

AMENDMENT WINS IN NEW JERSEY

Easy Victory in Assembly 46 to 5—Equal Suffrage Enthusiasm Runs High

The New Jersey Legislature passed the woman suffrage amendment in the Assembly last week by a vote of 46 to 5. The Senate had already voted favorably 14 to 5.

A large delegation of suffragists crowded the galleries, and when the overwhelming vote was announced there was a scene of great enthusiasm. Women stood in their seats and waved handkerchiefs and "votes for women" flags and cheered themselves hoarse.

Dr. Jekyll Becomes Mr. Hyde

Opposition was confined exclusively to the old sentimental arguments.

(Continued on Page 79)

MICHIGAN AGAIN CAMPAIGN STATE

Senate Passes Suffrage Amendment 26 to 5 and Battle Is Now On

Michigan is again a campaign State after a short lapse of four months. The amendment will go to the voters on April 7. The State-wide feeling that the women were defrauded of victory last fall will help the suffragists.

The final action of the Legislature was taken last week, when the Senate, by a vote of 26 to 5, passed the suffrage amendment, with a slight amendment to make the requirements for foreign-born women the same as those for male immigrants.

Governor Watches Debate

The debate in the Senate lasted an hour and a quarter, and was characterized by the persistent efforts of Senator Weadock and a few others to tack on crippling amendments. Several suggestions, including the disabling of women for holding office or serving on juries, were voted down in quick succession.

Gov. Ferris was among the visitors who crowded the chamber and gallery. Mrs. Clara B. Arthur, Mrs. Thomas R. Henderson and Mrs. Wilbur Brotherton, of Detroit; Mrs. Jennie Law Hardy, of Tecumseh, and other State leaders were present, supported by a large delegation of Lansing suffragists.

The final stand of the opposition was made by Senator Murtha in the hope of putting off the submission till November, 1914, and this also failed.

Of the five who opposed the measure on the final roll-call, three were from Detroit.

A complete campaign of organization and education has been mapped out by the State Association. The

(Continued on Page 74.)

General Rosalie Jones in Pilgrim Costume; Miss Inez Milholland on White Steed Leading the Parade; One of the Scores of Imposing Floats; One View of the Procession

This newspaper reported on the violence during the 1913 parade.

Nurses march in the Woman's Suffrage Parade in 1913.

The Time Has Come

Women had fought long and hard for the right to vote. Some had been jailed, and others were beaten. But, they never gave up. They remained strong and carried on the fight.

Their hard work began to pay off as more and more people began to change their minds. The suffragists started to convince more people that women should be allowed to vote.

On January 20, 1918, the Nineteenth Amendment was brought before Congress for the third time. Women were nervously waiting. When it got one more vote than the two-thirds it needed to pass, the women screamed and cheered in the streets. The *New York Times* newspaper reported that the celebration sounded like fans "after a football victory."

But, the movement was not over yet. The states still had to pass the law, and to do this, 36 states needed to agree. The last state to agree was Tennessee. People for and against suffrage came to watch the vote. Tennessee voted in favor of women's suffrage. The Nineteenth Amendment had finally passed!

On August 26, 1920, the Nineteenth Amendment became a law in the United States. The battle was won, and women could now vote!

H. J. Res. 1.

Sixty-sixth Congress of the United States of America;

At the First Session,

Begun and held at the City of Washington on Monday, the nineteenth day of May, one thousand nine hundred and nineteen.

JOINT RESOLUTION

Proposing an amendment to the Constitution extending the right of suffrage to women.

Resolved by the Senate and House of Representatives of the United States of America in Congress assembled (two-thirds of each House concurring therein), That the following article is proposed as an amendment to the Constitution, which shall be valid to all intents and purposes as part of the Constitution when ratified by the legislatures of three-fourths of the several States.

"ARTICLE ——.

"The right of citizens of the United States to vote shall not be denied or abridged by the United States or by any State on account of sex.

"Congress shall have power to enforce this article by appropriate legislation."

F. H. Gillett

Speaker of the House of Representatives.

Thos. R. Marshall

Vice President of the United States and President of the Senate.

For and Against

Michigan, Illinois, and Wisconsin were the first to pass the law. Georgia and Alabama were the first to reject it. The antisuffragist movement remained strong at this time. There were both men and women who were still against women's suffrage.

Listen to Your Mother

It was a close call in Tennessee. It was up to Harry Burn, a 24-year-old legislator who had always voted against women's right to vote. His mother urged him to vote for suffrage. At the last minute, he decided to listen to his mother and break the 48 to 48 tie.

Paul sews a star on a suffrage flag for each state as it ratifies, or approves, the Nineteenth Amendment.

Glossary

abolitionists—people who fight to end slavery

amendment—an official change to the United States Constitution

anniversary—the date which an event took place in a previous year

article—a separate part of a document that deals with a single subject

ban—to not allow

convention—a formal gathering of members

custody—to have legal control of a child

deny—not allow

federal courts—a national court established by the government

hunger strikes—refusing to eat for social or political reasons

illegally—forbidden by laws or rules

inauguration—a ceremony that occurs when a person is sworn into office

investigation—looking into something to find the facts

legislature—a group of people with the power to make and change laws

lobby—a group of people who try to get laws made that will help them

majority—a percentage greater than half of the total

militant—forcefully active in a cause

mobs—a large rough and loud crowd

opponents—people against something

permit—a written statement of permission

petitions—requests to change something

picket—a type of protest in which people march in front of a building and try to stop people from entering

plight—a bad condition or state

property—something that is owned like land, goods, or money

Quakers—members of the religious group called Society of Friends

sue—to seek justice from a person by bringing legal action

suffrage—the right to vote

suffragists—people who thought women should be allowed to vote

Supreme Court—the highest court of the United States

tactics—planned actions or procedures that result in an advantage or gain

temperance—the use of little or no alcohol

Union—the Northern states in the United States that were against slavery during the Civil War

universal—all people; everybody

vindication—to be free from guilt

Index

Your Turn!

At the start of the 1900s, American women were not allowed to vote. A group of female leaders worked hard to change that. In 1920, the Nineteenth Amendment gave women the right to vote.

Poetic Justice

One stanza of a poem is printed on the suffragist poster above. Add to the poem by writing three more stanzas. Follow the same rhyme pattern and give more facts and details about the Women's Suffrage Movement.